I0419585

Raccoons
For Kids

Amazing Animal Books
For Young Readers

By
Rachel Smith

Mendon Cottage Books
JD-Biz Corp Publishing

Read More Amazing Animal Books

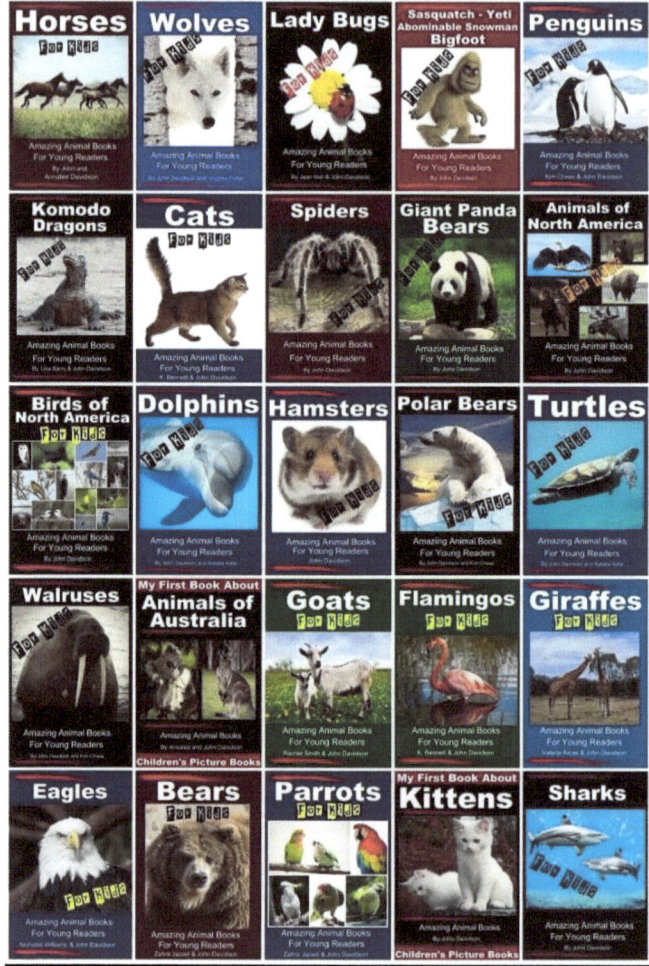

Table of Contents

Introduction

Raccoons are often referred to as little bandits due to the 'mask' on their face. And in some ways, this is a good description. They do indeed take things from human garbage and scavenge. But there is so much more to the raccoon.

The raccoon has not always been a scavenger of human trash, and that is definitely not their only role. They are interesting creatures full of history and quirks, and have long been part of native cultures in North America.

There is less variety to the raccoon than other creatures, such as dogs or cats, but there is a uniqueness to it. The raccoon is an ingrained part of American, Canadian, and other North American cultures.

What is a raccoon?

A raccoon is one of the members of the Procyonidae family. This family includes other creatures too, such as coatis, kinkajous, and various other new world creatures. A raccoon is a specific species of the genus Procyon, and a member of the superorder Carnivora.

A pair of raccoons.

The raccoon is the largest member of its family, which goes to show that members of that family don't get that big. It is an omnivore, which means they eat small animals, plants, and bugs.

Raccoons are covered in gray fur. This is also made up of dense underfur, which keeps the raccoon warm in the winter. Since they live as far north as Canada, this is very important for their survival.

They also have a ringed tail, and is shown to be closely related to ringtails, which are the two species the ring-tailed cat and the cacomistle. It was originally thought that raccoons were most closely related to coatis, but this is not the case.

The name 'raccoon' comes from a Native American name for it, from the Powhatan culture. There were and are a lot of other names for it, however. Some names include *Suksuk* (Miskito), *Touaru* (Choco), *Culu* (Mayan), and *Mapachitli* (Nahuatl, or Aztec). The Spanish took the Aztec name for the raccoon and called it *mapache* (among other things), though the French Canadians copied the English and called it *raton*.

Raccoons are very intelligent, and have been shown to remember how they solved a problem for a few years after they learned it. They also have dexterous hands that can do almost anything a human can do.

There is a much closer relationship between raccoons and bears than there is between weasels and raccoons. However, weasels and raccoons do have a lot in common. Bears and raccoons may have come from a common ancestor millions of years ago, and it is through this that they are related.

One animal that is not as closely related as some people think is the red panda. With its ringed tail and similar, though redder, appearance, it would seem like the red panda is closely related. However, this animal, while related, is distantly related.

There are about twenty-two subspecies of raccoon. This is mostly because different raccoons in different areas develop in different ways. For instance, a lot of the Florida Keys raccoons are pale-colored and have a less pronounced mask.

Some kinds have bigger skulls, or heavier teeth, or darker fur. Sometimes they are smaller than other raccoons, and other times they have flatter skulls. It can be any number of small differences that make them stand out.

Raccoons are generally about 40 to 70 centimeters. They are a medium-sized animal, and they have tails that are 20 to 40 centimeters. These ringed tails are often what make most people think of raccoons.

The males and females are somewhat different sizes, with the males being a bit bigger. However, this is the main difference between them in appearance. A raccoon often weighs twice as much shortly before winter as compared with spring; this is because the raccoon puts on fat to survive the winter.

It's thought that the mask on a raccoon, or the dark patches around its face, are so that they can see more easily in the dark. The idea is that the dark color doesn't reflect light, and so it reduces the glare around their eyes.

Raccoons are also covered in stiff guard hairs. Guard hairs are a part of the coat of an animal that protects the rest of the fur or body. These guard hairs help get the moisture, or water, off of the raccoon's body, keeping it dry and warm. They are often gray, and sometimes brown.

The raccoon has a small area of their skull for their face, but they also have a large brain case. It's pretty large in relation to the rest of the skull, and it's presumably this large brain that helps it have the intelligence it has.

The most important sense for a raccoon: the sense of touch. They have incredibly sensitive hands or front paws, which have a horny layer (material rather like horns) over the top. The horny layer gets pliable (easily bent and such) when it is wet.

They don't see colors well, but their vision is very good in the dark.

As said, they are very intelligent, and when tested to unlock locks, they could unlock most of them in fewer than ten tries. They remembered how to do it when the lock was moved or flipped upside down too.

How do raccoons act?

Raccoons can stand on their back paws to look at something in their hands. This is unusual for a creature of their type. They also can climb down trees face first due to being able to rotate their feet, something that most animals of their size cannot do.

A raccoon sitting and eating.

They also tend to move sort of slowly; their legs are short, so they can't run very fast or jump too well. They typically move on all fours, but have been seen to hold something in their hands and walk on their back legs.

Raccoons can also swim, able to stay in the water for hours swimming at a kind of slow speed.

This type of animal lives sort of in groups. The females tend to live in a common area, only coming together for things like feeding. Raccoon females are fairly social.

Males, on the other hand, tend to gather in loose groups so they can fight off other males when it's mating season. They don't have quite the closeness of the females.

There's one last way raccoons live: the mother females tend to live by themselves with their kits. Kits are baby raccoons. This is because sometimes other male raccoons will attack kits, and the mother keeps them separate until they can defend themselves so they don't get hurt.

However, this idea of raccoon society is a bit challenged. Some zoologists say that raccoons are mostly solitary creatures, and actually don't live in groups. The more prevalent belief is the first one, however.

Raccoons mark their territory with their scents. This territory is usual double the size for adults than it is for juveniles, or not quite fully grown raccoons. However, as long as there is enough food, it doesn't matter much to the raccoons if their territories overlap a little. Sometimes, during mating season, overlapping territories become a point of contention, and raccoons will fight over it.

The raccoon tends to be active at night. Sometimes, however, they'll be up during the day to take advantage of food sources. The raccoon is possibly the world's most omnivorous animal. An omnivore eats almost anything edible, which for the raccoon meant an almost even split between things like bugs, small animals, and plants. This is also why they get into people's garbage so much: there's so much of what they eat there!

Dousing is something that most humans think raccoons do all the time. It means that a raccoon will 'wash' its food, or stick it in water. It's even a part of its scientific name, Procyon lotor, lotor meaning 'washer.'

One theory is that raccoons do this to wet their paws, which makes them more sensitive. This has been mostly debunked, or proved not to be true. Another theory is that they are descended from animals that mostly ate seafood, and so this mimics (acts the same as) fishing for small seafood.

Another theory was that they don't produce enough spit in their mouths to swallow things. This was proved wrong some time ago.

The most common and earliest theory is that the food is dirty and they're cleaning it, but that is not the case. Raccoons will take food that isn't dirty and stick it in dirty water to douse it. No part of the dousing seems to involved cleaning, even though they do take parts off of the food after they've doused it.

But the thing is, only captive raccoons have ever been seen to douse. Wild raccoons, in their natural habitat, have never been seen dousing their food. In fact, the idea that wild raccoons do it has been called into serious question.

This mistake is a lot like the mistake made with wolves in captivity: when wolves were first captured and observed, it was assumed there were Alpha wolves that controlled the pack, and lower wolves were not treated well. But the problem with this assumption was that wolves actually live in family units, and the wolves captured were just a bunch of frightened, unrelated wolves who naturally acted hostile towards each other to survive.

What does that prove? That captive animals often act in ways that are not natural to them. Similarly, dousing may be a captive animal action, and not a normal raccoon behavior.

Mating is a big deal for raccoons. Typically, during the mating season, a male will roam his territory, looking desperately for females to court. The female will only be able to have a baby with him during a span of three to four days, so he has to court her fast.

Even the weak male raccoons in their group will get to mate. It's just that the strongest will mate more often and have more potential mates. There are typically more than enough potential mates for either sex.

Female raccoons typically have anywhere from two to five kits, or baby raccoons. They carry them for about two months before giving birth, meaning that the babies are born sometime around abundant summer. Finding food for the babies is not much of an issue for mothers in this season.

The more likely it is for a raccoon to die of something that isn't old age, the larger the litter of kits. For example, in North Dakota, they tend to have more, and in Alabama, less (these are a northern state and a southern state in the United States of America).

Kits are born deaf and blind. However, the mask that sets apart raccoons is already visible at birth, so a raccoon kit is easily recognizable. About twenty days later or so, their ear canals open, and then their eyes not too long after.

Kits must grow to be about one kilogram before they leave the den where they grew up with their mother. This is only to explore, however, because it's pretty dangerous out there for new kits. After about sixteen weeks, they stop nursing and by the fall, they tend to split up.

Males go much further away than females; this helps stop inbreeding, which is when closely-related animals have babies together. This can be bad for any group, including humans.

Where do raccoons live?

Raccoons live in many places. The main one is in the New World, or the Americas. Naturally, raccoons occur everywhere from Canada in the north to Panama down south.

A raccoon in a forest.

Hispaniola, the island that makes up the two nations of Haiti and the Dominican Republic, was entirely robbed of raccoons. Back before 1513, Spanish settlers ate all the raccoons. This is a common thing in Hispaniola, where much of who and what lived there were made 'extinct.'

In Jamaica and Cuba, the raccoon was also exterminated by the same forces: hungry Spanish settlers. However, the ecosystem and the peoples living there were not quite as destroyed as in Hispaniola.

Raccoons living in the United States and Canada have increased their population since the 1930's by almost twenty times. This explosion of raccoons is due mainly to the food left out in garbage, which is much more full of calories than their typical foods. This means it makes it easier to survive, and so less die, and even more are able to reproduce.

They have also spread to other parts of the world. Thanks to people either not keeping them captive or releasing them on purpose during the 20th century (the 1900s), raccoons now live in several European and Asian countries. The biggest population in the world outside of the Americas is in Germany, where there are many sightings.

There was a series called Rascal the Raccoon in 1977 in Japan. This led to many, many raccoons being imported as pets, because it was a very popular show. Unfortunately, thanks to many of them escaping, there is now a large population of raccoons in all 47 prefectures in Japan.

Raccoons were actually intentionally released into the wild in Germany. Several people who wanted to enrich their fauna (make it more interesting, better game for hunting, etc.) tried to introduce it, but the raccoon population did not take hold.

After that, they caught on. A second population started when a bunch of them escaped from a fur farm (a farm where animals are grown to be used for fur) because of a bombing during World War II.

Now, raccoons are spread throughout Germany, and are considered a game animal where they were once protected.

One last place that needs to be talked about was called the Soviet Union. This was a sort of empire that Russia, Belarus, Azerbaijan, Latvia, Lithuania, Estonia, Ukraine, Moldova, Armenia, Georgia (the country, not the state in the USA), Kazakhstan, Kyrgyzstan, Tajikistan, Turkmenistan, and Uzbekistan were all stuck in.

The history of the Soviet Union is fairly complicated, and now all these places are their own countries, but at one point they were one country. This country tried to make Communism work, and it failed.

One attempt to provide more fur and food for the people in the Soviet Union was to release raccoons into the wild. They tried many times to get them to live in the sometimes harsh environment, but most of the time, the raccoons died out.

However, in Belarus, a population caught on. In Azerbaijan, they really caught on, and about a thousand are caught every year in that country, providing food and fur. The area of Dagestan (which is part of Russia today) had some success with raccoons as well.

Most of the times that raccoons were introduced to the environment in these countries, it was done out of a thought to improve things. People thought that having an animal that made good fur and was okay to eat was a good thing. However, introducing an animal to a foreign environment can be very bad.

For example, take a look at the ball pythons in Florida in the United States of America. They grow enormous with no predators and eat pets.

Or, a more extreme case: rabbits in Australia. There are so many rabbits in Australia that they destroy natural habitats of other animals and eat their food. Nothing eats rabbits in Australia, so it's been up to Australians to try to keep their numbers down.

As far as can be told, the raccoon has not been nearly as disastrous to its new homes as the rabbit was for Australia. But it is still a risky business to bring exotic animals to a place with no predators.

The history of raccoons and humans

Raccoons and humans have a long history.

A raccoon trying to get into trash cans.

The native peoples of North America have long had mythologies and stories about raccoons. Often, they are presented as tricksters. In other stories, they are presented as wise beings, because their masks are similar to the face paint used in some ceremonies.

The Aztecs believed female raccoons had supernatural abilities. This is because they saw the way a mother raccoon cares for her babies, and saw this as very similar to their wise women.

Most of these groups hunted the raccoon for its meat and fur. This was sustainable, and the raccoon was doing all right.

Then the Europeans came, and all bets were off. Not only did they wipe out raccoon populations in some areas, as before mentioned, but they hunted in big numbers in other areas as well.

Early American settlers relied a lot on raccoons and other animals to clothe themselves and eat. This was a huge source of food for those who settled in California, and it was fairly expensive for the time.

While it was not considered cheap or poor people food, raccoon was sometimes served for Christmas for African slaves back when slavery was legal.

Raccoons suffered a huge hit when, in the 1920's, raccoon fur automobile coats became all the rage. Automobile coats were large, covering coats that people wore when they drove cars, because in the 1920's, cars did not have tops, and one would get almost covered in dust and the like.

The book *The Joy of Cooking*, a famous cookbook in America published in 1931, actually had a recipe for raccoon.

In the 1930's, as the money that could be gotten for raccoon skin seriously dropped, the hunting slowed down. The raccoon got the chance to revive its numbers.

Right around this time began the urban raccoon. Raccoons, since at least the 1920's, have been attracted to the easy food in our garbage cans.

Some raccoons are so used to humans, they don't even run when they see them. They've been known to steal and eat dog and cat food, though they won't eat dogs and cats, generally speaking.

Sometimes, people feed the raccoons on purpose. This is not a good idea, as it's not really healthy for them to live on people's garbage. However, this urbanization of raccoons has led to a boom in numbers, and there is no danger for this animal right now.

Extinct raccoons

There are two known kinds of extinct raccoons.

First, there is the short-faced raccoon. This one existed during the Pleistocene era, which was a very long time ago. The main difference between it and modern raccoons was the short face and robust teeth.

A more recent subspecies of raccoon that's now extinct is the Barbados raccoon. This one lived in Barbados up until about 1964; its problem was that it was a small population, isolated from other raccoons, and so inbreeding and dwarfism was very common. This led to them being too weak to continue to survive, and the last known one was hit by a car in 1964.

Crab-eating raccoon and Cozumel raccoon

There are two other kinds of raccoon other than the main kind, the common raccoon described in this book. The first one is the crab-eating raccoon, and it lives in mostly South America.

Not surprisingly, it eats crabs and other animals, and bears a strong resemblance to the common raccoon. Unlike the common raccoon, it doesn't like to come into human spaces all that much, and sticks to riversides and other places like that to live.

The Cozumel raccoon is very endangered. It lives on Cozumel Island off the coast of Mexico, and is also known as the pygmy raccoon due to its size. It appears the Maya, a people who lived in this area long ago, used to eat raccoons of this size.

The main threat to the small Cozumel raccoon is tourism. The tourism takes over the island and makes it more difficult for the raccoons to live. They are critically endangered.

Conclusion

Raccoons have long been the masked thief of the night, but there is so much more to this animal. Not only is not a hissing, terrifying beast, it's an animal that is made to adapt to all kinds of settings.

The raccoon is an amazing creature, and we would do well to learn to adapt as well as it does.

Author Bio

Rachel Smith is a young author who enjoys animals. Once, she had a rabbit who was very nervous, and chewed through her leash and tried to escape. She's also had several pet mice, who were the funniest little animals to watch. She lives in Ohio with her family and writes in her spare time.

Publisher

JD-Biz Corp

P O Box 374

Mendon, Utah 84325

http://www.jd-biz.com/

Horses
For Kids
Amazing Animal Books
For Young Readers
By John and
Annalee Davidson

Ponies
For Kids
Meridian Cottage Books
Amazing Animal Books
For Young Readers
Rachel Smith

Ten Amazing Horses
For Kids
Nature Books for Kids
JD-Biz Publishing
K. Bennett

Akhal-Teke
"The Golden Horse Of the desert"
For Kids
Nature Books for Kids
JD-Biz Publishing
K. Bennett

Suffolk-Punch
"The Gentle Giant"
For Kids
Nature Books for Kids
JD-Biz Publishing
K. Bennett

Shires
"The great Horse"
For Kids
Nature Books for Kids
JD-Biz Publishing
K. Bennett

Colonial Spanish
"Horse of the Americas"
For Kids
Nature Books for Kids
JD-Biz Publishing
K. Bennett

Canadian
"The Little Iron Horse"
For Kids
Nature Books for Kids
JD-Biz Publishing
K. Bennett

Cleveland Bays
"History and Future"
Horses For Kids
Nature Books for Kids
JD-Biz Publishing
K. Bennett

Raccoons

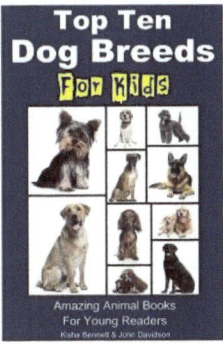

Top Ten Dog Breeds For Kids

Amazing Animal Books For Young Readers

Kisha Bennett & John Davidson

German Shepherds

Dog Books for Kids

K. Bennett

Bulldogs

Dog Books for Kids

K. Bennett

Dachshund

Dog Books for Kids

K. Bennett

Poodles

Dog Books for Kids

K. Bennett

Labrador Retrievers

Dog Books for Kids

K. Bennett

Rottweilers

Dog Books for Kids

K. Bennett

Boxers

Dog Books for Kids

K. Bennett

Golden Retrievers

Dog Books for Kids

K. Bennett

Puppies

Dog Books For Kids

Amazing Animal Books

By John Davidson

Beagles

Dog Books for Kids

K. Bennett

Yorkshire Terriers

Dog Books for Kids

K. Bennett

Dogs

Top Ten Dog Breeds For Kids

Amazing Animal Books For Young Readers

Zahra Jazeel & John Davidson

Cats For Kids

Amazing Animal Books For Young Readers

K. Bennett & John Davidson

Foxes For Kids

Amazing Animal Books For Young Readers

Zahra Jazeel & John Davidson

Wolves For Kids

Amazing Animal Books For Young Readers

By John Davidson and Virginia Fidler